SUMMARY:
12 RULES FOR LIFE

AN ANTIDOTE TO CHAOS

BY JORDAN B. PETERSON

EXECUTIVE**GROWTH**
SUMMARIES

D1444154

For those who dare ask more, learn more, and become more.

TABLE OF CONTENTS

BACKGROUND

Jordan B. Peterson is a clinical psychologist from Canada. He is a professor of psychology at the University of Ontario, and more recently, he has become something of an Internet celebrity, in large part because of the success of the book this summary is based on, *12 Rules for Life*.

The journey that led to the writing of this book started as series of posts on the internet forum Quora, which allows users to answer questions that have been posted by other users. The author was surprised at how much interest his answers were generating on Quora, and so he was encouraged to start writing a book that allowed him to dive much deeper into his original rules for life.

Politically speaking, the left has called Peterson a right-winger, while the right has called him a left-winger. What are his views? Peterson puts it this way:

"...Temperamentally I am high on openness which tilts me to the left, although I am also conscientious which tilts me to the right. Philosophically I am an individualist, not a collectivist of the right or the left. Metaphysically I am an American pragmatist who has been strongly influenced by the psychoanalytic and clinical thinking of Freud and Jung."

Perhaps balance and common sense rank high on his list of priorities.

The 12 Rules are an attempt to condense a lifetime of learning into a pragmatic antidote for chaos. Throughout the book, Peterson sees *Chaos* and *Order* as the two opposing principles that rule all of life, reigning over simple life forms such as lobsters, to the most complex of all, human beings. Chaos means the unknown, calamity, suffering, and disorganization. Lies, half-truths, and ignorance fall into this category too. On the other hand, there can also be such a thing as too much order. Peterson tells us not to interfere with kids when they're skateboarding for exactly that reason. Discipline may have its place, but we also need to leave room for growth, exploration, and pushing the limits.

In Peterson's view, the trick is to negotiate the abysmal border between order and chaos (like yin and yang) in a balanced and harmonious way.

He is, above all, forthright and direct in how he approaches every Rule for Life. He's also unafraid to stir up controversy when speaking about liberalism, Marxism, or about social injustice. Growing up in the frigid wastelands of Northern Alberta made him tough enough to face life head on, without fear, and without sugarcoating anything – something of that spirit shines through in each Rule.

The advice is pragmatic and based on the real-life struggles of ordinary people facing the chaotic totality of life. The rules offer practical advice and insight into the complexity of the human mind. They can also be used as a compass to help anyone find his or her proper direction in life – an antidote to chaos.

Our team has distilled the essence of the full work, while remaining as true as possible to the original without plagiarizing the content. We have singled out the key concepts and trimmed out all the rest, allowing you to digest the author's core message in a fraction of the time. Within each rules you will also find "**Rules in Action**" where we interweave the dense, theoretical advice with relatable stories.

POWER INSIGHTS

As our valued reader, we cherish your time and focus. When reading the following **Power Insights** you will instantly capture the key learning points of *12 Rules for Life*, create an effective mental map of the book, and better retain the remainder of the summary.

***

Jordan B. Peterson grew up in a remote town in northern Canada called Fairview. It was a cold and unforgiving place – the kind of town that breeds a doughty spirit. In the book *12 Rules of Life*, we get a glimpse into the author's personal world, and we follow the development of his recipe for mental and emotional well-being as it unfolded in his mind and heart over the course of his life.

Peterson went on to become a professor of Psychology and later something of an Internet celebrity with *12 Rules for Life, an Antidote for Chaos*. In the book, he traces some of the events in his life that shaped his world-view. He also sets out on a few forays into the metaphysical labyrinth from which his *Rules for Life* spring.

Rule 1: STAND UP STRAIGHT WITH YOUR SHOULDERS BACK. It might sound like old-fashioned common sense – and in fact, many of the rules do – but there's a lot of research and original thought behind each one.

Dominance hierarchies have existed on Earth since the formation of the first organisms. In slightly more complex creatures, dominant males get the best mates, the best territories, and the best food – while those on the bottom rung must struggle to survive. It's nature's response to the chaos of non-existence, part of the very fabric of life, and it's hard-wired into the nervous system of most living animals, including human beings.

Our biological hardware rewards us for survival with feelings of well-being, increased levels of Serotonin, and better health. We have a kind of primordial calculator deep in our nervous systems that keeps track of our relative place on the hierarchy. If we understand this, Peterson argues, it gives us the opportunity to leverage knowledge. A good posture and a winning attitude gives a clear signal to ourselves and others that we are in a good position (within the hierarchy) regardless of where we may actually stand. Our posture declares that we are not scrapping by on the low rungs of society and in turn allows for greater chances of success – which may actually translate to material, upward movement. However, our decision necessarily means that we are responsible for facing the weight and facts of life head on.

Rule 2: TREAT YOURSELF LIKE SOMEONE YOU ARE RESPONSIBLE FOR HELPING. Instead of being your own worst enemy, or living as a martyr and putting the needs of others above your own needs, it's important to look out for yourself. In this section, the author goes deeply into the origins of guilt and feelings of unworthiness. Peterson traces our shame back to the universal myths of original sin and man's relationship with God and the world at large. He argues that most of us would go to great lengths to look after another person who happens to be in our care (like our own children), so why not treat ourselves with the same care?

Rule 3: MAKE FRIENDS WITH PEOPLE WHO WANT THE BEST FOR YOU. The third rule is illustrated by stories from Peterson's past in which he shares how some of his best friends spiraled down into empty and meaningless ways of life. He investigates the motives of those who try to play the hero to failing friends, even though they are dragged down in the process. He discusses the dynamics of poisonous relationships – the kind that eventually derail your life without adding anything to it. Real friends want what's best for you – they're not afraid to use tough love if need be.

What kind of a relationship do you have with your own inner critic? **Rule 4** advises you to **COMPARE YOURSELF TO WHO YOU WERE YESTERDAY, NOT TO WHO SOMEONE ELSE IS TODAY**. Here, Peterson examines the nature of perception and shows us how we're all vulnerable to blind spots in our thinking and perception. We see only what we believe or what we expect to see. We're often blind to our own faults – but when they are revealed, we're too hard on ourselves. We compare ourselves to others who are better at one specific part of life than we are, and then we blow it all out of proportion.

Instead, we can learn to change the way we look at things. We can attend to today's problems as best we can and keep struggling to be better than we were yesterday – without comparing ourselves to others.

Rule 5 deals with the challenges of parenting: **DO NOT LET YOUR CHILDREN DO ANYTHING THAT MAKES YOU DISLIKE THEM**. The road to parenting hell is paved with good intentions, Peterson says. He illustrates how parents who treat their kids like "little Emperors," or those who allow too much freedom for their children, are inadvertently creating their own worst nightmares. Nobody likes a brat. Would you rather protect your child from life or make them strong enough to deal with it effectively? Keep the rules to the absolute minimum, but be consistent, and use only the minimum necessary force – but discipline your kids. They'll thank you for it later.

Rule 6 deals with a fundamental existential dilemma: How do we respond to *Being* in this world knowing full well the horrors, disappointments, and joys it contains? There are some who decide that life is meaningless and that it isn't worth the effort. Then there are those who persevere through the ordeals they are dealt through life and decide the opposite: Life is what we make of it.

However, before you go off and take on the ordeal of making the world a better place, remember to **SET YOUR HOUSE IN PERFECT ORDER BEFORE YOU CRITICIZE THE WORLD**. Like Aleksandr Solzhenitsyn, who lived through the horrors of the Soviet Gulag day-by-day and learned from his trials. Solzhenitsyn's book helped dismantle Communist Russia, but he first had to set his own house in perfect order.

Rule 7: PURSUE WHAT IS MEANINGFUL (NOT WHAT IS EXPEDIENT). Our consciousness gives us the ability to think things through, to decide what we want (or need) and to go out and get it. It is both a blessing and a curse. Each of us carries within us the potential for great good and great evil. Each of us needs to consider what is worthwhile pursuing in life. Sacrifice is never easy – even when we know that a small sacrifice today means a better tomorrow. The highest wisdom is to live a life that fills you with a sense of meaning instead of pursuing only what is expedient in the short term.

Human beings are incredibly resilient. We can withstand hardship and survive terrible tragedy – but only if we safeguard our characters, keeping them strong and authentic. Lies are devastating because they wreak havoc on our relationship with reality. Small lies turn into big lies until eventually it becomes impossible to tell the difference. Our psychological integrity depends on an authentic, honest approach to life. **Rule 8 is therefore: TELL THE TRUTH—OR, AT LEAST, DON'T LIE**.

Rule 9 deals with the art of genuine conversation. That means learning to listen, above everything else. As a psychologist, Peterson has found this rule of life particularly rewarding. In this chapter, he points out that nobody can have a meaningful conversation if the goal of the conversation is only to get the other person to accept your ideology – in other words, to win the argument. Instead, if we learn to listen to the other person and listen to ourselves as we speak, we begin to see that we're organizing our thinking by talking. Other people are like mirrors – we can see ourselves reflected in their responses, in their body language, and in their reactions. This is different from preaching or winning a debate. In other words: **ASSUME THAT THE PERSON YOU ARE LISTENING TO MIGHT KNOW SOMETHING YOU DON'T**.

Sometimes we sweep things under the rug, hoping that the problem will go away. Of course, that doesn't usually work. People multiply their problems when they avoid talking about them. **Rule 10 is BE PRECISE IN YOUR SPEECH** for that very reason.

By speaking precisely, you can pinpoint any problem. You can identify it, bring it out into the open, and do something about it. If you remain silent, or worse, if you argue about vague generalizations or unspecified negative emotions, the problem can grow. Be forthright, honest, and direct about what it is you want – spell it out clearly to those who need to know.

In the author's view, life exists as a dynamic interplay on the border between chaos and order. **Rule 11** elaborates on this point. Throughout the book, this idea surfaces as a theme, and he discusses the idea from different angles. One aspect of this interplay is the fact that life becomes boring when people are not challenged – when too much order stifles our creativity and our spirit. Kids and adults alike will seek out challenges in order to grow and evolve. That's why teenage boys will slide their skateboards down the railings of staircases. They're willing to take the risk because they want to be better skateboarders. Should we enforce endless rules just to keep them safe? No, says Peterson. **DO NOT BOTHER CHILDREN WHEN THEY ARE SKATEBOARDING**.

The final rule for life, **Rule 12,** implores the reader to **PET A CAT WHEN YOU ENCOUNTER ONE ON THE STREET**. In other words, remember that life is not just about the struggle – there's wonder in it too.

It is the struggle to exceed our limitations that ultimately brings meaning to our lives. Even superheroes need limitations and challenges; otherwise, we wouldn't read comic books. In the final chapter, Peterson shares the heart-wrenching story of his own daughter's trials through a debilitating health condition. At one point, he wondered to himself how life could be so cruel to an innocent child. But the conclusion he came to was this:

> *"When you love someone, it's not despite their limitations. It's because of their limitations."*

Each of us carries our own burdens through life – and there's more than enough misery to go around. Small acts of kindness can remind us that life is worthwhile – if you meet a cat on the street and it rubs against your leg, remember to pet it. It's a reminder that there is a little bit of wonder in the world too.

***

If you enjoyed the **Power Insights** and want to keep a copy as a reference or to share with your friends and family members, feel free to download your exclusive digital copy by scanning below.

Follow the steps below to instantly access your exclusive Power Insights guide for *12 Rules for Life*:

1) **Open** your smart phone's camera application

2) **Aim** your phone's camera **and focus on** the QR Code below

3) **Click** the link that pops up on the top side of your screen

Or by following this link in your browser:

https://exegrowth.com/pdfguide-12rfl-04

Now get ready to uncover a new understanding of effective human psychology that very few hold. See you on the other side.

RULE 1:
STAND UP STRAIGHT WITH YOUR SHOULDERS BACK

Rules in Action: Introduction

There's a Law of Nature that every lobster knows: The dominant male gets all the girls.

Take Louis, for example. Louis is an average lobster, at best. He's blessed with middle-of-the-pack genes, and although they keep him from the bottom rung of lobster society, he also remains far from the top. Louis is not exactly the alpha male, and he is in a constant struggle to maintain his place in the middle.

He can fend off smaller lobsters, but he shies away from conflict with those that are bigger than him and this makes him stressed, tired, and weakened. But Louis is lucky. He's a member of a species that has thrived for 350 million years, and presumably, that gives him a little bit of confidence.

Waking up one day and poking his head out from under his rock, he sees another lobster approaching. This lobster is Rex. Rex is older, bigger, and a rung higher than Louis in their little community. Louis knows what's happening. Rex wants his shelter and Louis has to make a decision – fight or flight.

*

Posture is a looking glass. In the first chapter of his book, Jordan Peterson analyzes how something as seemingly straightforward as posture indicates one's status within their dominance hierarchy.

If you observe a lobster, you will find that it has complex behavior patterns, and like most other creatures in nature, it has to fight to defend its territory, to claim the best mating partner, and to secure its relative place in the food chain. **Strong, dominant males attract all the girls, lord over the best territories, and get to eat the best foods.** That's a Dominance Hierarchy.

Hierarchies serve an essential function in nature because they bringing order to chaos. These hierarchies have shaped living organisms for millions of years As a result, living creatures are designed to crave and obsess over **status and position,** which inevitably creates **conflict**.

Competing individuals need to find ways to assert their dominance without risking serious injury in physical combat – hence, the signaling power of status and position.

Competitive and dominance behaviors are hardwired into lobsters' nervous system, just as they are wired into the brains of wrens that must fight to defend their nesting territories. Even chickens in captivity must establish their own hierarchies – the "pecking order." These behaviors are also wired in human beings. **Ancient evolutionary structures in our brain** keep tabs on our ability to survive in different environments and subsequently suggest our place within the dominance hierarchy – like a primordial calculator. In other words, **defeat and victory have a direct impact on our neurochemistry.** They are both fundamental drives that humans have inherited.

When a strong lobster defeats a weaker lobster, something weird happens. The brain of the weaker lobster dissolves and it grows a new one that is more suited to its subordinate position. The ratio of two chemicals, serotonin and octopamine, regulate the balance. High serotonin levels go along with victory, flexed pinchers, strong posture, and cocky behavior. High octopamine usually means defeat and results in a lobster that looks crumpled and puny by comparison. **It's interesting to know that serotonin plays a similar role in the human brain.**

This subtle brain chemistry ensures that winners are more likely to win in the future, while losers will continue to lose. **The Principle of Unequal Distribution** (Price's Law or Pareto Principle) comes into play. For instance, the rich get richer while the poor get poorer; a small number of cities contain most of the people in the country; and only a handful of individuals rise to the top spots of any hierarchy. This cumulative feedback is another trait nature has developed to bring order and propagate life, ensuring the survivability of successful individuals, and hence the descendants of those successful individuals and so on.

The Victorian idea of evolution is that it is a straight line with steady and continuous development due to natural selection. But this doesn't fit perfectly with observed reality. The "nature" that selects is itself subject to change, meaning there are no straight lines. To quote Peterson:

"Nature dresses differently for each occasion."

Humans have shaped, *and are shaped by,* their social environment, and like any other natural environment, it has a **Top and Bottom.** Our primordial brain calculators receive signals from our higher brain functions as to where we are and where we want to be on that hierarchy.

With these principles and the way we're wired, we become entwined in **either positive or negative feedback loops**. If you have poor posture, for example, you're signaling to others that you are defeated and you're inviting people to treat you like a loser. If you straighten up, people will treat you differently.

> *"To stand up straight with your shoulders back is to accept the terrible responsibility of life, with eyes wide open."*

In short, when you stand up straight with your shoulders back three things happen immediately:

First, **you are choosing to face life head on and accept full responsibility for your actions.** This decision itself will boost your confidence as you mitigate the effects of randomness and assert control over your day.

Second, **your body's archaic hormonal system will respond by secreting more serotonin**, readying itself for the path ahead with renewed vitality and vigor. You will feel physically better as a result.

Third, **your posture will indicate to others around you that you are a winner.** They will take notice and treat you accordingly.

The three of these reactions set you up for greater chances of success and reinforce a positive feedback loop. The more your chances of winning, the more you win. The more you win, then simply...the more you win.

So don't hold back, straighten up, and express your desires. Accept adulthood with all its challenges. Face the uncertainties of life with courage and fight back against the chaos of defeat and destruction. **Choose to do that which is a trait of success even if you haven't yet achieved that success.** Anxiety will drop away, social acuity will heighten, and you will be better equipped to tackle your own destiny. **Stand up straight with your shoulders back.**

*

Rules in Action: Application

Rex continues to approach the shelter. Louis does some quick calculations and reckons that his odds of winning might increase if he appears larger or simply more confident than he feels at the moment. So, he straightens up and faces Rex squarely. The two of them jockey for position, analyzing each other and their odds of success. Rex is an older lobster on the way out, and he has been falling in rank lately. This attack on Louis is a desperate action fueled by the stress of octopamine.

Rex lunges desperately but misses. Louis is younger and faster. This emboldens Louis and he moves toward Rex. The confidence radiates from him. The surrounding lobsters take notice. Louis isn't such a pushover after all.

Rex backs away slowly, flooded with the stress of defeat. On the other hand, Louis has learned a valuable lesson and earned a higher rung, retained his shelter, and gained a better mate too.

RULE 2:
TREAT YOURSELF LIKE SOMEONE YOU ARE RESPONSIBLE FOR HELPING

Rules in Action: Introduction

"I know you think what you're planning on doing is right," said James, *"but can't you see that it's eventually going to make you bitter, resentful and cruel? In fact, as far as I can tell, it's already happening. You're so miserable these days, it's getting hard to be your friend."*

"But if I go away to study, who is going to look after them?" Simon replied, carefully keeping his voice low so neither his younger brother nor his father would overhear. He always seemed to be doing that.

James looked over to where Simon's father was watching television. Beer cans littered the coffee table, as usual, and the old man was barely awake by now.

Simon held a letter in his hand, and he was reading it again for the umpteenth time. It informed him that he had been accepted for an engineering scholarship. If he accepted, he would have to leave his father and brother to fend for themselves – something that he just couldn't bring himself to do.

> *"I'm no more important than they are. I'm nothing."* Simon
> *said those words so softly that it could scarcely be heard.*
> *"There are so many people who deserve this more than I do."*

*

"It is not virtuous to be victimized by a bully, even if that bully is oneself."

Why do people think that it's acceptable to treat their pets with more compassion than themselves? Even chronically sick people will sometimes care so little for their own health that they disregard their doctor's advice and skip their medication. Strangely enough, if a vet prescribes medicine for their sick dog, the same person will make sure it's administered properly.

Do people loathe themselves on some deep, fundamental level? Could the reason for that be fear or shame? Why do some people seem so hell bent on self-destruction?

In this chapter, Peterson delves deep into the mythical drama of creation as it is recorded in the Bible to illustrate how our experience of being alive is like walking **a fine and dangerous line between chaos and order**. Much of the world we know is predictable, stable, and known. But we also sense an unknown, chaotic underworld that constantly threatens to break out of the order and overwhelm us. It's the fear of this unknown element that makes us behave in ways that are not good for others or ourselves.

In Genesis, God the Father (representing Order) is said to have used the Word (*Logos*) to create and structure the known world out of chaos. He placed Adam and Eve in Paradise. **The Garden of Eden was** a stable, orderly, supportive, and life-giving place. But just outside the gates, chaos lurked.

When the primordial couple tasted the fruit of the knowledge of good and bad, they symbolically became **conscious**. Using their mind's eye, they could now see the future approaching, and it wasn't all sunshine and roses. They became aware of their own mortality, unlike the other animals.

Even more alarming, their faults and shortcomings now became obvious to them. Their vulnerability made itself known. **They became aware of the chaos surrounding them, and as a result, they felt naked and afraid.** The couple felt unworthy and ashamed to stand before God.

Adam blamed Eve, who in turn blamed the serpent. The worst possible "snake" of all is not a literal one but the all-too-human tendency toward fear and evil. It is an internal, psychological thing, and each of us carries a part of that chaos within us. No walls can keep it out.

That deep sense of shame, confusion, and unworthiness brought on by our aptitude for consciousness lies at the heart of all our self-destructive behavior. It's why we won't do what's good for us. Each of us knows better than anyone else the flaws, inconsistencies, and inadequacies that are hidden within us.

Humans also have a capacity for wrongdoing and deliberately inflicting pain on other living things that is unmatched by anything in nature. **Do humans deserve to exist at all? Perhaps man is something that should never have been.**

In the Taoist tradition, order and chaos are represented by the symbols of Yin and Yang. Yin is the Feminine; it is chaos, matter, and the unknown. Yang is masculine; it represents order, hierarchy, and the known. This philosophy also points to the best, or the only, proper way to live – negotiating the fine line between these two extremes. To accomplish this, we need to be truly conscious with eyes wide open.

The original pre-thinking humans may have enjoyed the bliss of ignorance, but their eyes were not open. In that sense, at least, we're better off than they were. As difficult as it is for us to bear the burden of consciousness, at least we have free choice. Isn't it better to "walk with god," or in other words, live in the proper way, even though we're fully awake, conscious, and aware of our in-built propensity for evil? That's better than self-division. It's better than self-destruction too.

If you're a parent who is responsible for looking after a child, you naturally have to consider what is ultimately best for the child. You teach, encourage, admonish, and help. You care for the child's basic needs. You help the child become conscious, strong, virtuous, and courageous. You make sure they brush their teeth and wear warm clothes when it's cold outside.

What would your life look like if you cared for yourself with the same diligence, intelligence, and effort as you would your child?

How would your life look like if you treated yourself as if you deserved your best efforts? Because you do. What is the alternative?

What career would you choose if you truly loved and cared for yourself? What bad habits would you immediately annihilate? What goals would you set? What new habits would you form? What new hobbies would you take on?

Don't underestimate the power of your vision and direction. Take care of yourself as if you were someone you were responsible for helping.

*

Rules in Action: Application

"You deserve the chance to make something of yourself, my friend. Don't let it slip away." James had a fierce look on his face as he spoke. "At some point you're going to have to realize that you deserve your own help, and you don't have to let them hold you back. You'll be sorry if you do. I know you want to help them, but maybe the best way to do it is to help yourself first."

The intensity of those words hit home, somewhere deep in Simon's mind and heart. The more he thought about his motives, the clearer it all started to become. He was playing the role of the dutiful older son, the martyr, and his father and brother were only too happy to play along.

What James was saying was right on the money. Simon was already becoming bitter and resentful, and he was far too young for that.

"It's not easy to love yourself." Said Simon, with a wry smile.

"I know," James smiled, "But you've got to start somewhere."

RULE 3:
MAKE FRIENDS WITH PEOPLE WHO WANT THE BEST FOR YOU

Rules in Action: Introduction

"Are you coming?" Lucy called back to Andrea, who was still sitting under the tree, reading.

"What are you guys going to do tonight?" Andrea called back, putting a long leaf in the book to mark her place.

"The usual, I suppose. Ben and his friends are coming with his dad's pickup. Maybe that cute friend of Ben's will be there."

"Those guys are bad news," Andrea said, still deciding whether or not she was getting up. She was reading Notes from Underground by Dostoevsky and she was just starting to enjoy it. She watched Lucy walk back to where she was sitting. *"All they ever do is talk about cars and get stoned."*

"What's wrong with getting stoned?" Andrea laughed and changed her voice teasingly. *"Are you too good for that now? Is it going to interfere with your college plans?"* The last part was said with more bite than the first.

"It probably will. You know it's what I'm intending to do. Why are you giving me a hard time about it?" Andrea asked, trying hard to keep the irritation out of her voice. She picked up her book again. A shadow of emotion flickered across Lucy's face and suddenly she was mad as a hornet.

"You're just pretending that you're better than us!" She yelled, and with that she stormed off down the path, as Andrea looked on. "Suit yourself, miss 'A' Student." Lucy called from a distance. "You're missing all the fun!"

*

Fairview, Alberta is a cold and unforgiving place to grow up. Peterson amusingly describes the hardships that people, and pet cats alike, had to face in the bitter winters of the far north of Canada. Cats would unwittingly crawl into the engine compartments of parked cars, seeking warmth. It often happened that the driver would start the engine before the cat had left and then things would get ugly.

If the frostbite and the cold didn't get you, the sheer lack of stimulation would do the trick. That was the kind of place Fairview was. The closest city was Edmonton, 400 miles away. Some of the kids who grew up in Fairview knew they would eventually leave. They knew it from early on. Others knew they would never leave.

The Fairview Teenage Wasteland mostly consisted of driving aimlessly around town, getting drunk, or going to some dismal and slightly creepy house party. In a place like that **it's easy to choose friends who aren't good for you**.

Watching some of his closest friends slowly and deliberately spiral into meaningless, repetitive, and broken lives was one of the hardest lessons Peterson learned to deal with. He described his friend's choices and life trajectory as a "*Motivated* refusal to learn."

"Chris" was a bright kid, but he kept choosing the wrong friends and allowed himself to be dragged down. He somehow developed a low opinion of his own worth. Perhaps he simply refused to take responsibility for his life.

When people do this, they tend to choose new acquaintances exactly like the people who dragged them down in the past. Apathetic friends will tend to grind each other down by default unless someone makes the choice to escape the poisonous environment and work toward improvement. The fact is that down is easier than up. It's easier not to think about your life and not to care. Chris took the easy way out, and sadly, he never reached his potential.

Peterson advises that before you decide to **play the hero and rescue the dammed,** like someone (even a close friend) whose life is out of control, it's wise to ask yourself why that person is in trouble. Is he a victim of circumstance or is it by choice? **It's a noble thing to want to help, but not everyone who is failing is a victim; many times they are failing by choice. And they can't help but drag you down with them.** It might even be your own vanity and narcissism that makes you think you're the hero.

It's also easy to delude yourself about why you stay in an unhealthy relationship. Is it truly self-sacrifice, or is it because you're too weak-willed and indecisive to leave?

When you surround yourself with people who encourage and support your highest goals and aims, they won't let you self-destruct or go off the rails. They will bolster you, encourage you, and gently counsel you when you make a mistake, just as you would do for them. Choose to surround yourself with people who want the best for you.

*

Rules in Action: Application

In the weeks that followed, Lucy and Andrea began to drift further and further apart. Andrea felt terrible about it, but

Lucy had gotten it into her head that Andrea was being condescending and judgmental. She started bad-mouthing Andrea among their friends, causing things to get worse. Finally, Andrea couldn't stand it anymore and she confronted Lucy, hoping to rescue the friendship and rescue her friend from making terrible choices.

"How long have we been best friends? Is it seven years?" She started, as calmly as she could.

But it was no use. Lucy didn't want to hear it and pushed her away harder than ever. It was clear that their paths were diverging.

By the time Andrea finished college and moved to New York, they had all but lost touch. From time to time, Andrea's family sent her news about Lucy's downward spiral. But all she could do was watch from a distance. There was no going back, but she knew she'd made the right choice.

RULE 4:

COMPARE YOURSELF TO WHO YOU WERE YESTERDAY, NOT TO WHO SOMEONE ELSE IS TODAY

Rules in Action: Introduction

"Look at this. What do you think the latest status symbol must have cost? Look at him posing next to it."

Marco leaned over to show his wife a photo on his phone. His boss was standing next to his new Ski Nautique speedboat. The look on Marco's face was a mixture of envy and self-loathing. A deep crease appeared between his eyes.

"You know I've been at the company just as long as he has, but there he is with a new boat and a lake house while I sit here in a tiny two-bedroom apartment. What's wrong with me? How come he gets all the luck? Am I destined to be a loser forever?"

"Your turn will come, my love." Melissa feigned disinterest in the photo but she was more concerned about the look on her husband's face than she let on. Why was he so unhappy? "Besides," she added, almost as an afterthought, "Didn't you say you thought his wife was cheating on him? At least you've got me."

Marco pulled his eyes away from his phone to look at Melissa. Something about the way the light was catching her hair reminded him of the first time they had met. All their experiences together flooded his memory in waves of warm emotions. She was right, of course. He didn't even like boats. Why was he making himself miserable about it?

*

Inside each of us, there's a relentless voice that condemns our mediocre attempts to rise up the ladders of success in life. Our **internal critics** can be ruthless – they can turn us into our own worst enemies.

Add to that the interconnectedness of today's world. We can now compare ourselves to billions of other people, and of course, quite a few of them are going to be more talented, more capable, or simply better than us. The voice in your head loves to point out those facts.

It's complicated because we know that **the same internal voice can be useful in many ways**. The same voice helps us make value judgments and lift our standards. High standards are necessary unless you want to stay trapped at the bottom. But the trouble is too often that critical voice simply won't shut up.

Life engages us in many different games. Some we win, but others we lose. Even if we're temporarily winning at everything now, it also means we're not growing as much as we could, or would like to, in the long run. As we mature and grow, we each have to decide what we genuinely want, what we're willing to sacrifice, and how much reward we need to receive so that we don't feel like beasts of burden in our own lives. None of us want to be obedient lapdogs to any tyrant, even if the tyrant is us.

Can we learn to get along better with that critical voice in our head?

In this chapter, Peterson argues that it is possible to change that internal dialogue from a destructive one-way criticism into a fruitful two-way discussion. Turn that critic into an ally, he advises. The author recommends that we start by taking stock, as it were, of our lives and asking ourselves some tough and probing questions: "Who am I really?"

Call upon your inner voice respectfully, and with sincerity. Ask it to help. Ask it to offer advice. Don't be treacherous with yourself either. Keep promises you make to yourself. More than likely, the inner voice will suggest something that can improve matters – something that you can set in motion without resentment. Keep at it, day after day, and keep holding up your end of the bargain with your inner self. Soon your habits will change, and you will constantly be in a frame of mind that asks: "What could I do to make my life just a little better today?"

An honest, in-depth review of your life can be a crushing, demoralizing, and lengthy operation. However, it can also be the start of a much-needed inner renovation. Dare to be dangerous and dare to be utterly truthful with yourself.

Many times what we must shift is our perception of reality and focus on the things we can control about ourselves. However, perception is tricky and is inherently tied to what we habitually focus on. Whatever we tend to focus on is our perception of reality; we are blind to everything else.

Cognitive psychologist Daniel Simons illustrated this more than 15 years ago when he recorded a video of six people playing a ball game near an elevator. Participants in the study were asked to watch and count the number of passes made by the team wearing white – the correct answer was 15. Then Simons asked:

"But did you see the Gorilla?"

Incredibly, about half the people who took part in the study failed to notice a fully grown man wearing a gorilla suit in plain sight during the game because they were so focused on their counting task.

Our eyes, along with the power of perception, are useful tools. But the price we pay for that vision is blindness to everything that we're not directly focused on. We see only what we want to see or expect to see. We're blind to the rest, and this is especially true when we look at our own beliefs, thoughts, and feelings.

Each of us looks at the world in our own particular, idiosyncratic way. We screen out most of what we see so we can detect the important details. It's a process that takes a lot of time to master, and eventually, it becomes completely habitual. That habit leaves blind spots, however. It's only when we become aware of our habitual way of looking at things that we can learn to change the way we look at things.

Life is never the problem – we are. When we look at it this way, at least we have options. **We can change our perception and look at things differently**. Perhaps that's what our inner critic has been advising all along. Perhaps our unrealistic longings and our immature desires are actually blinding us from what's really best for us in the long run.

Attend to the problems that each day brings while keeping your eyes firmly on the highest good you can see. Compare yourself to who you were yesterday, not to who someone else is today.

*

Rules in Action: Application

*"You look like the mouse that got away with the cheese,"
Melissa said, as Marco playfully tossed his car keys on the
counter. "Good day at work?"*

*"Awful." Smiled Marco. "In fact, I'm thinking about quitting."
A mischievous light danced in his eyes as he spoke.*

*Melissa froze midway between the dishwasher and the
cupboard with a stack of plates in her hands. "What did you
just say?"*

*"Remember I told you about Jefferson Consulting down on the
coast? Well, today Tony Jefferson himself called me and
offered me a job. Can you believe it? You always said you'd
love to live there. Wanna move?"*

*"I thought you'd given up on that and decided to stick it out
where you are. You said you couldn't hack it. What's
changed?"*

*"I know, but I've been doing a lot of thinking. I've been too
hard on myself and too scared to let go of this job — but I've
been selling myself short. My talents are wasted here."*

*Melissa put the plates into the cupboard and shut the door
with her foot. Thoughts were scrambling in her head, trying to
catch up with each other and she didn't know what to say
first.*

*"We don't have to decide right away," Marco said casually, as
he started helping his wife pack away the dishes. "But you
said you wanted a new challenge, and it's not as if we have
kids to think about. Why not?"*

Melissa eyed him skeptically. This was unexpected. Where was the usual miserable self-loathing? She still didn't know what to say but a calming smile soon appeared on her face as she kept her hands busy packing away the pots.

RULE 5:
DO NOT LET YOUR CHILDREN DO ANYTHING THAT MAKES YOU DISLIKE THEM

Rules in Action: Introduction

"What's the matter, Jim? You look like you didn't get any sleep. Hope it was for a good cause."

Mike chuckled as he held another board in place so Jim could fix it to the frame. Jim was clearly struggling to concentrate. "Maybe I should operate the heavy machinery today," Mike added.

"It's my kid, he's driving me nuts. He won't sleep." Jim passed the pneumatic drill over and took the board from Mike as they kept working.

"Your kids are all grown up now... How the hell did you manage?" Jim had to time his sentences between the bursts of noise from the drill.

"Jen and I argue about raising kids all the time," he continued when the noise died, "She wants to stimulate their creativity, give them space, and pamper the hell out of them, but I just want them to do as they're told. It's my son that's the worst. It takes me two hours every night to get him to fall asleep. Do the math – do you know how many hours of sleep I'm losing a year?"

"It was easier in my day, I will admit," replied Mike. "Then again, it's never easy. But Maggie and I learned a few tricks over the years. I'll share them with you over a beer some time. If you can make it through the day without stapling your own hand to this house that is." Mike laughed and jabbed Jim in the ribs, teasing him.

"Tell you what, why don't you bring Jen and the kids over this weekend? I know Maggie is going to whip up some of her famous apple pie."

*

There's a common myth that leads to a lot of misery in parent-child relationships. It goes something like this: "There are no bad children, only bad parents." Sometimes you'll hear a different variation of that myth: "When children misbehave, it's the fault of society at large, never the fault of the child."

There might be a grain of truth in those myths, but they paint a picture that is far too one-sided to be accurate. Instead, it would be better to say: **It's hard for any parent to strike the perfect balance between nurturing and enforcing discipline**. It's an art, and it takes effort to learn that art.

For his fifth life rule, Peterson calls on his years of experience raising his own children along with his experience in dealing with beleaguered parents in his capacity as a psychologist. He offers some balanced guidelines on how to approach this prickly aspect of life.

There are plenty of ways to get it wrong. Some mothers treat their sons like little Emperors of the Universe. Some fathers are terrified that their children will stop liking them, and so they **try too hard to be friends with their kids instead of being their parent**. Other parents just seem not to care. Instead of genuine concern and compassion, there is a deep, unconscious resentment, or even hatred, and the eventual outcome is never good.

Too much discipline will break a child's spirit, but too little, and the child becomes rotten. Where, exactly, is the golden mean?

Obnoxious children are an embarrassment and a disgrace to their parents. They can become so demanding of a parent's time and energy that they can suck the joy right out of life. Out of desperation, such a parent might eventually discipline their child too harshly. How can we prevent this from happening?

It's naïve to imagine that little children are all angels, that they contain nothing but good, and that left to their own devices they will bloom into perfectly well-adjusted adults. Kids crave the attention of adults and friends precisely because they need to be socialized. They need to *learn* how to be good, how to be capable, and how to be fair – it's not all instinct. Someone capable needs to show them how.

Young children will always try to push their boundaries just to see how much they can get away with. They will kick, hit, scratch, and bite when they don't get what they want, and they're perfectly happy to live on fruit loops and candy bars if given the chance. Most of them are one part angel and one part devil.

Every child deserves the chance to learn how to comply with the expectations of his social environment in a graceful way. That doesn't mean mindless conformity. It means that their parents use reward and punishment strategies wisely. They've thought long and hard about how to root out the kinds of behavior that will damage the child in the long run, and they've thought about how to encourage behavior that leads to a successful and happy life.

Here are some practical hints:

1) Keep the number of rules to a minimum, covering only what is essential. For example, don't hurt other people, stand up for yourself, eat in a civilized and grateful way, and learn how to share.

2) Be fair and consistent about what happens when those rules are broken. Start small by **using the minimum necessary force**. Learn by experimentation what forms of punishment work best for your individual child. A Time-out can be effective, especially if the child is welcomed back once he has mastered his or her temper.

The family institution is an ancient part of human life. It brings stability and order to life and provides a protective wall against the psychological chaos that lies outside. Children suffer more in the long run when their parents are inattentive and when they fail to teach them the skills necessary for life. Remember, nature and society will teach your child far harder lessons if you let your child manipulate you, or if you don't teach your child how to handle difficult situations.

When a child has learned from his or her parents how to pay attention instead of drifting aimlessly, when the child can play without whining, and the child can showcase a sense of humor without being annoying, social interaction becomes easy. There will never be a shortage of friends or adults who don't mind helping.

If you want your child to thrive, show them how to live in a way that doesn't make you dislike them.

*

Rules in Action: Application

Jim and his wife got back home from a lovely dinner at Mike's place - Maggie's apple pie was even better than Mike had promised.

Jim was feeling extra gracious from all of Mike's and Maggie's parenting advice and so he gave his niece an extra $10 for babysitting the kiddo, Tommy.

As usual Tommy was restless and wanted to keep playing computer games. "Time for bed," Jim announced from the first floor. But Tommy just kept playing.

"Tommy, time for bed, let's not do this again..." Jim's voice was starting to get more agitated when he recalled Mike's advice and instantly changed his tone. "Actually, I have something exciting to show you!" he exclaimed as he made his way upstairs. Tommy looked over his shoulder with his baby teeth showing and a sparkle of intrigue in his eyes.

Jim brought one of his favorite books when he was a kid and started reading to Tommy, just as his dad had done. He had forgot how nice it was to read to his boy. Tommy loved it.

"Dad...one more story please???" Tommy politely asked.

"Okay, one more but pinky promise we both go to sleep after. Deal?" Jim said with a soothing smirk.

"Deal!" exclaimed Tommy. After Jim finished reading "Jack and the Beanstalk" he tucked Tommy in and they both went to sleep shortly after.

"I can't believe that worked" Jim thought to himself. And with even more enthusiasm he found another adventure book for

the next day. Tommy preferred books with clear heroes going on treacherous pursuits.

For the next week Tommy would still make a case to stay up later but Jim made a simple rule: "If you are in bed by 9:30pm we will do story time. If not, you still have to go to bed with the lights out and no story time." Jim knew to be consistent with his rule, as Mike had advised him.

On Thursday night Tommy was not ready and much to his despair he would not get hear the new book Jim had built up. "But DAD!? Please!" Tommy shrieked. But Jim knew better to cave in or to be overly authoritative. Jim calmly hugged Tommy and said "Tomorrow be ready in time. Good night, I love you."

Tommy was ready at 9:28 the next day, tucked in and head perked awaiting his dad.

By the end of the month Jim had a system ready, he would recycle three books and find two new books for the week. Now story time was an activity they both looked forward to. Jim now had 30 minutes of uninterrupted quality time with his son instead of two hours of exhaustive struggle.

Everyone noticed Jim's renewed energy. His wife loved it, his boss loved it, and his colleagues loved it.

"Your advice was golden, I can't thank you enough" Jim exclaimed as he patted Mike on the shoulder. "Let's get beers after work. On me."

"Sure! That zombie Jim was dangerous around here. Glad to have you back." Mike heckled as they both arrived at the new construction
                                                                        site.

RULE 6:
SET YOUR HOUSE IN PERFECT ORDER BEFORE YOU CRITICIZE THE WORLD

Rules in Action: Introduction

"Why should I bother?" Gary sneered, tossing his history of economics textbook across the room. "Why should I waste one miserable minute on studying this rubbish? It's brainwashing!"

"Don't you want to earn your degree? Why did you enroll?" Joan was getting bored listening to Gary's tirade. He had been complaining about the world for an hour, and it seemed like he was just getting started.

"Earn a degree? That's exactly what I mean. The whole system is corrupt and unfair. The banks create money out of thin air to keep the nation in debt. The leftists want to spend it all on social reform, which means looking after bums and losers who are too lazy to work, while the rest of us have to bust our asses in permanent debt. Meanwhile, our politicians are taking money under the table and the people making the guns are getting rich and fat."

"Well, Gary," Joan sighed, "Don't study it then. But if you'll excuse me, I intend to graduate next year, so I'm going to work now." She put her headphones in her ears and opened her book. Gary was still fuming about something that

bothered him, but she didn't care to listen anymore. Why was she with him anyway? Putting the thought out of her mind, she found the page she wanted and continued reading.

*

We all know the terrible cliché: "Life sucks, then you die," and perhaps even worse, we've all felt that way at some point in our lives. It's true: Life can seem unfair, meaningless, cruel, and empty. However, the unanswerable question remains: **who is really to blame?**

In classic literature, you will find many stories that have mankind's unbearable existential suffering as a central theme. Mephistopheles, the devil in Goethe's *Faust,* for example, says: "I am the spirit who negates, and rightly so, for all that comes to be deserves to perish, wretchedly. It were better nothing would begin!"

The author goes as far as to examine the mindset of sociopaths, such as the Columbine killer who said: **"The human race isn't worth fighting for, only worth killing."**

We can understand the way he feels, to some extent. But is it fair to condemn the human race to extinction because life is hard or because it's unjust? Peterson juxtaposes that mindset of despair and vengeance with the story of **Aleksandr Solzhenitsyn (sohl-zh*uh*-neet-sin)**.

Solzhenitsyn fought in the trenches when the Nazi forces invaded Russia. He was arrested, beaten, and thrown into prison – not by the enemy, but by his own people. He ended up in a Soviet labor camp, enduring horrendous conditions during the best years of his life. But the hardships didn't stop there. He was later struck by cancer.

During his stay in the Gulag camp, he came across people who endured the torture of imprisonment in a noble way. They said "yes" to life, despite the horrors they endured. It made an impression, and he started to question his own motives and his own way of thinking. He thought deeply about the mistakes he had made in his life. He pondered over his failings, and began to ask himself: **"Can I repair the damage? Can I stop making the same mistakes now?"**

He recorded his honest thoughts and his unvarnished experiences in a book: *The Gulag Archipelago*. The book was banned in the USSR. Even so, it made it to the West, where it exposed the truth and became instrumental in demolishing the credibility of the communist system. It helped to dismantle the oppressive regime. One man's courage and honesty helped to free millions from suffering.

In this life, suffering is unavoidable. It's bound to come your way. No sane person can look at the world and honestly believe that people are perfect or that life is just roses. When the suffering goes beyond a certain point, though, when it becomes too much to bear – **all you can do is examine your own response.**

"Don't blame capitalism, the radical left, or the iniquity of your enemies. Don't reorganize the state until you have ordered your own experience. Have some humility."

Peterson argues this way: Before placing all the blame on God, on society, or the human race, think for yourself: **Have you cleaned up your own life?** Have you used every chance you were offered? Or are you allowing a sense of bitterness to rob you of even the possibility of peace? Do you have habits that are ruining your health? Is there something that you know you should do or that you could do that could alleviate some of the suffering?

If you allow your soul, or your highest self to guide you, then small, incremental changes will add up over time. Eventually, things might not be quite as tragic. If nobody allowed the weight of the world to quench their drive to be their best, imagine how much better life could be.

We can all agree that there is much to criticize in this life – but before we do that, let's set our own house in order.

*

Rules in Action: Application

"Have you heard from Gary lately?" Joan's mom asked, as she rolled up the window. They were driving back from dinner on the last night of her visit in Joan's college town.

"I haven't spoken to him in months. You know he dropped out, right?" Joan said. She loved chin-wagging with her mother. It had been far too long since her last visit, and it was a treat to catch up.

"I know, you told me a while ago. That's why I asked."

"Last I heard he was trying to get into Greenpeace. I don't know if they will accept him without a degree, though."

"Well, that's positive, at least." By the tone of her mother's voice, Joan could tell exactly what she really meant. The first time Joan had introduced Gary to her mother, she'd figured him out in only a few minutes. Mom was good like that.

"I can't believe I stayed with him for almost a year. What was I thinking?"

"We're all young and stupid once." Her mother said, smiling faintly. "So long as you learn from your mistakes and make better choices next time."

"He was getting so dark toward the end. I thought he might buy a gun. I think this Greenpeace thing is just another way to take revenge on the world. Did you know he wanted to go to Afghanistan and join ISIS at one stage? Thank heavens he didn't take to Islam. Before that it was socialism. Or was it something else? I forget."

"Really? I know he liked to complain about life a lot. I didn't think it was that bad. Well, anyway, I'm proud of you, my daughter. You've made good choices, mostly."

Joan looked carefully at her mother, searching her face for cynicism or irony. But her face was open and truthful.

"I don't need to change the world." Joan said. "I'll just work on myself instead." She turned the radio up loud as a catchy pop song came on. Mother and daughter sang their hearts out to the cheesy lyrics all the way back to the parking lot.

RULE 7:
PURSUE WHAT IS MEANINGFUL
(NOT WHAT IS EXPEDIENT)

Rules in Action: Introduction

Sandy walked over to the musician as he was packing up his gear. She'd been waiting for a chance to speak to him since the first time she'd seen him. She approached him timidly but caught his attention.

"I just wanted to thank you," She said. "I've seen you here three weeks in a row, and what you're doing for these kids is so great. You really cheer them up."

"Thanks," he replied. "My name's Harry, by the way."

"Sandy." She smiled as they shook hands. "You're really good – are you a professional entertainer?"

"More or less," Harry laughed. "But I don't get paid to play here. I do it because I want to. I love seeing these kids smile." The last of the children were wheeled back to their rooms. Two or three of them had shaved heads – the telltale signs of chemotherapy. Others pushed their drip stands along in front of them.

"I always wondered..." Sandy continued, "What makes you do it? Where do you get the energy?"

Harry finished packing and looked at her seriously for a moment.

"Why don't I buy you a cup of coffee and I'll tell you about the most important decision in my life?"

*

"Meaning is when everything there is comes together in an ecstatic dance of single purpose."

If existence, life, and the universe are ultimately meaningless, what difference does it make how we live, what we choose, and who we become?

We can all agree that it's painful to exist as a conscious being in this world. Therefore, isn't it better to be a complete hedonist and pursue nothing except what brings pleasure? **Isn't it better to simply do what's expedient** – in other words, whatever works, without bothering to think about a higher meaning?

A wolf in the wild that makes a kill will eat 20 pounds of meat in one go as quickly as it can because another animal might come along at any moment and take his meal away from him. Humans have learned that there's a better way. Somehow, over untold centuries, we learned that **if you sacrifice some of what you might eat today, there will be more to eat tomorrow**.

It took even longer for us to distill that core idea into a meaningful story and refine that story through painful experiences. Sacrifice is an ancient idea. Humans made sacrifices to their gods, hoping to gain something out of the deal in the future. The amazing thing about it is that sometimes it worked.

In this chapter, Peterson examines the stories that shaped our ideas about sacrifice. The story of Cain and Abel in the Bible is one example.

God seemed to prefer the sacrifices of Abel over Cain's, and it all had to do with the intentions behind their sacrifices. The story of the sacrifice of Jesus is another example.

Modern man now has the privilege of knowing **the thoughts, actions, and decisions of today shape the structure of tomorrow's reality**. We've risen above practicalities, and to be fulfilled, we feel the need to pursue a sense of meaning in our lives.

The fundamental notions of Time and Causality are deeply intertwined in the idea of sacrificing something today to make tomorrow a better place – even if you're not around to enjoy it. **The trouble is nobody can make himself or herself act wisely today by simply making an intellectual decision to do so.** Anyone can say: "I will stop smoking," or even, "I will not procrastinate." Unfortunately, it's easier said than done. Unless you honestly understand yourself, you're doomed to fail.

It is only once you confront your own propensity for evil, along with your own vulnerability, that you begin to see how vulnerable everyone and everything else is too. To find a sense of meaning, you need to confront your true nature and dig into your painful past.

The author goes on to share some of the details about his own search for meaning brought on by the "dark night of the soul" he lived through as a young man. He wanted to find a fundamental truth that was beyond all doubt. He wanted to find something that felt real.

For Peterson, the answer was that suffering is the ultimate human reality. Nobody can deny that life is hard, and that we all suffer. This is something everyone can understand directly, *a priori* (something that is known before it is seen). The worst kind of suffering comes from humans who willfully inflict pain on others. That's pure evil.

Each human being carries inside them the capacity for evil – but also for good. Good means whatever stops evil things from happening. In Peterson's view:

> *"the central problem of life—the dealing with its brute facts—is not merely what and how to sacrifice to diminish suffering, but what and how to sacrifice to diminish suffering and evil—the conscious and voluntary and vengeful source of the worst suffering."*

Striving only for what is expedient is narrow and selfish. It is immature. Striving for meaning, on the other hand, takes maturity. When you can regulate your impulses, you can begin to organize and unify your thinking with your deepest nature. Then you can begin to think about values. If your value structures are aimed at the betterment of your own Being, and of those around you, the revealed meaning you find will become life-sustaining. It can become an antidote to chaos and suffering.

Your **psychological integration** depends on aligning your thoughts and actions to your deepest values. If you're willing to shoulder the burden of existence, knowing full well how painful it is, you can begin to see things differently. You notice things that cause pain that you're able to fix, and you fix them.

Having a deep sense of meaning is better than having possessions or getting what you want. You probably don't even know what you want. It comes down to making the decision: There's no point in resenting *Being*, even though it's hard.

From there, the next step is obvious. You can think about how to best spend your time making things better instead of worse.

*

Rules in Action: Application

"I was 30 years old," Harry was saying, "When it suddenly struck me that my life was completely meaningless. I went through a painful divorce, and I looked at my life and didn't like what I saw."

"I'm sorry to hear that," said Sandy, sipping her coffee. "What did you do?"

"First, I took some time off work to think about things. Not easy to do when your boss makes you work 80 hours a week and you're handling millions of dollars. I was a career man – my job meant everything to me."

"So why did you quit?"

"It was a sacrifice – I won't lie. I had to give up all the luxuries I was used to, and there have been times when I've been flat broke. But I never regretted it."

"Was it always your dream to be an entertainer?"

"In a way it was my dream. The thing is – at that time in my life I had two choices: Keep doing what I was doing and remain miserable or change and lead the kind of life that felt meaningful and worthwhile."

Sandy put down her cup and placed the spoon in the saucer. Her mind was racing. On some level, she knew exactly what Harry meant – for she was feeling the same sense of meaninglessness in her own life.

"You've actually given me a lot to think about, Harry." She sighed.

"Well, that's a good thing, isn't it?" His eyes twinkled with compassion and friendliness. "I've got to go – but I hope I see you here again next week?"

"You can count on it." Sandy said. A smile bubbled up from somewhere inside, splashing across her face.

RULE 8:
TELL THE TRUTH—
OR, AT LEAST, DON'T LIE

Rules in Action: Introduction

Rafi always avoided talking to people on long-haul bus trips. He'd done his fair share of commuting across country, and usually he liked to just stare out the window and think his private thoughts.

But Hellen, the elderly woman who sat in the seat next to him this time, was different. She was neither nosey nor a constant talker. There was something wise and graceful about her, and not in a pretentious way. Above all, she seemed authentic.

Without realizing how it happened, he'd started talking about his deepest fear – telling his parents that he'd dropped out – and now the sluice gates were open and the words were gushing out.

"If I tell them, it will break their hearts. You don't understand what they've sacrificed to give me this opportunity," Rafi explained. "My father came here from Bangladesh without a penny to his name. Both my parents worked their entire lives to send me to college."

"So you think a little white lie is better than telling the truth?" Helen asked. There was no trace of judgment in her voice – Rafi could tell that she only wanted to understand him better.

"My parents have always made good choices for me. I can't disrespect their wishes – they're counting on me." Rafi said,

> *trying to contain his emotions. "But I'm not a dentist, and I never will be, no matter how much I try to force it. Something in me refuses to do it."*
>
> *"You're not a child anymore, Rafi." Hellen said gently. "What does your own heart say is best for you? You can lie to them, but you can't lie to yourself."*

*

We're all familiar with cold, hard truths. We also know all about half-truths, white lies, and even blatant lies. Most adults know exactly how to use words in subtle ways to manipulate the world in order to get what they want. Quite a few kids are pretty good at it too.

We know what's politically correct and what isn't, and we're all too familiar with the tactics of salesmen and pick up artists. But **we're not always good at spotting the lies we tell ourselves, especially the fundamental ones**. In this chapter, Peterson discusses life choices that go a lot deeper than telling simple lies.

In his view, **there are two diametrically opposite ways to exist in this world: One is living the truth and the other is taking the easy way out by living a life-lie**. The first approach takes courage, and it's difficult. But living a life-lie is worse because it undermines you in every way.

"Life—lie" is a term coined by Alfred Adler, who was a psychologist and a peer of Sigmund Freud. It describes someone who manipulates reality (lives a lie) in order to achieve some personal aim. It is someone who pretends that he is working insane hours to give his family a better future, for example, when in reality it's all about pride or ambition. It is someone who uses crafty arguments to justify their ideologies, just to prove themselves right, or someone who behaves falsely to ensure that everyone likes them. It's when someone **gets stuck on a fixed, pre-defined view of reality instead of remaining open to the complexities of the truth.**

Every time you act out a lie to save face, get something, or avoid conflict, you weaken your character. If you have a weak character, when adversity appears you won't be able to stand tall. Instead, you'll hide, and when you discover that the lies are catching up to you, you might end up behaving in terrible ways. **Lies are a pathway to the Hell of self-division.**

Lies start out small – the tiniest of lies are where the biggest lies start. We sense those lies inside of us, maybe in the pit of the stomach. If we're alert, we can feel them divide us and make us weak. Hell begins when things start to fall apart and when the **lies begin to corrupt the relationship we have with reality itself**.

If your character remains strong, authentic, and intact, you can weather the worst of life's storms. Human beings are incredibly resilient when they are upright, honest, loving, and authentic. When deceptions start to slip in, what follows is absolute ruin. When your life is a lie, there are no solid foundations anywhere.

How do you react when you don't get what you want out of life? Do you automatically feel that the world is unfair or that it's someone else's fault? Or do you honestly question your own methods, accepting that you still have something to learn? The first approach is based on a lie; the second is authentic.

When you stay truthful, your values transform you as you progress through life. You then have a proper relationship with the things you don't know. In other words, you admit your ignorance honestly and are open to learn from it. **If, on the other hand, you decide that your**

rational mind already has all the answers and you've already discovered all the important facts – that's totalitarianism. In Peterson's view, this is the source of all the suffering of mankind.

Every new bit of learning is like a miniature death. **When we learn that our old-world view is wrong, we need to let it go and rethink our ambitions in the light of the new truth we discover**. The old truth dissolves and chaos appears in its place, which is painful and scary. It takes an act of faith to trust that your *Being* can be corrected, that it can become something new and better. Truth can become deeper.

It is our responsibility to confront life in truth with courage and then learn from it, even if it seems horrible. **To live the truth means to bring the best version of reality to the light**. Your own personal truth is something only you can discover. Dig it up, articulate it, and communicate it carefully to yourself and others. Don't be afraid to challenge it. If your life is not what you imagine it should be, if you feel lost or confused, or if your sense of meaning seems confused, try telling the truth – or at least, don't lie.

*

Rules in Action: Application

"Where are you, Rafi? What does that strange look on your face mean, my love?"

Rafi pulled himself back into the present moment and smiled. He took his wife's arm and teasingly pulled her down onto the couch with him.

"I was just remembering something I haven't thought about in years. Lost in thought!"

"Oh, really? Do tell!" She giggled.

"I was thinking about what a wise, old woman once told me on a bus long ago." Rafi said, as his wife curled up next to him. "I've told you about the time I dropped out of college – you remember?"

"I remember. Your dad almost killed you that day. It must have been so hard for you both."

"It was," Rafi said. He felt a tinge of the pain he remembered responding somewhere inside. "But in a way, it was the best decision I ever made. It taught me something about life that's worth more than all the money in the world."

"And what might that be? Or is it a secret?"

"It's no secret. I was living a lie – and that lie would have ruined me, and it would have been much worse for my family in the end. My father couldn't see it at the time. He wanted me to be a dentist ever since I was 10. I don't even know why – that's just what his idea of 'success' was."

"But you're a successful businessman now – can't he see that?"

"He does admit it – now. But it took years for him to accept it."

"Well, I'm glad the two of you sorted it out."

"I never could have done it if it wasn't for that conversation on that bus – all those years ago. I remember it so clearly. It was the first time I actually looked at things honestly – and it was such a relief to finally tell my parents. As tough as it was, it was the start of a better life. More honest, you know?"

"I get that, and I'm proud of you, Rafi. I would never have married a man that was living a lie – so it's just as well you got your act together in time!"

"Lucky me!" Laughed Rafi. "I wonder whatever happened to that woman – Hellen – I believe that's her name. She will never know how important that conversation was."

RULE 9:
ASSUME THAT THE PERSON YOU ARE LISTENING TO MIGHT KNOW SOMETHING YOU DON'T

Rules in Action: Introduction

"Last week, just before our session ended, you told me that you felt like a stranger when you spoke to your husband. Do you recall? I'd like to pick up from there. Would you mind?"

Sharon crossed her legs defensively, as she sat on the couch.

"I don't know how it happened," she hesitantly replied. "We used to talk and talk when we first met. Now we hardly have anything to say. It always seems to end up as an argument."

*

There's an art to having a genuine conversation. Part of it is the way we talk, and the other part is listening. The real secret lies in **the way we listen**. As a psychotherapist, Peterson has had to deliberately and conscientiously work on it. With this Rule for Life, he shares some valuable advice on how to master the art of listening.

Throughout the chapter, he illustrates what he has learned by sharing the stories of some of his patients. Sometimes all Peterson had to do was to actively listen, as the patient talked about their dilemma and even talked through what they were planning to do about it. The only thing the patient needed was the chance to talk it through honestly and without judgment. **As they talked, they were *listening* to themselves think.** But those were the exceptions. Usually, there needed to be more interaction.

Sometimes it took a long time for him to figure out what the other person was trying to say. It was as if the person was struggling to articulate their ideas for the first time. He compares it to someone who places a stack of hundred dollar bills onto the table. Some of the bills are real and some are counterfeit. The only way to know what's really on the table is to go through the entire stack, note by note, and to diligently compare the differences. It's the same with the stories we collect about ourselves. **It's only when we lay it all on the table that we can carefully begin to separate the truth from delusion.**

Our memories are inaccurate, and **every time we talk about the past, the past changes slightly**. Each time we relate the story of our life to another person, we decide what to forget and what to hang on to – the story changes. But as it changes, we're also working things out in our heads.

As a psychotherapist, Peterson had to learn to assume that the person he was listening to knew things that he didn't (especially things about themselves). Sometimes he needed to offer advice, but mostly it was about understanding the worldview of the other person. Above all, **he learned not to impose his own ideologies** onto his patients. Instead, he would allow them to own their problems and own their journey to recovery.

We organize our thinking by talking things through, even if it's just in our heads (internal dialogue), and we definitely need to think about our lives unless we want to blindly stumble into every pitfall along the way. In order to properly think things through, we need to allow room in our heads for at least two opposing worldviews. It's not easy;

it takes effort to be clear, articulate, and fair. That's why having a high quality conversation with another person is so valuable. **It's also useful to take what the person has just said to you, formulate it in your own words, and repeat it back to them so you know you're both on the same page.**

Even if the person you're talking to doesn't say a word, that person is testing you and testing your thinking. In a sense, the listener represents all of humanity and common sense.

As we talk about our experiences, we simulate the world and visualize how our plans will play out in the real world. This allows us to see where we could fail using the power of imagination (and the input from the other person). **This helps us avoid stupid mistakes, or at least learn from them so we don't repeat them.**

There are other ways to have a conversation, but they seldom lead to personal growth. When one person is talking to dominate the room and establish his or her place in the dominance hierarchy, it means they're not listening. Some people talk *at* you, and when you speak, they're only thinking about what they're going to say next to top whatever you're saying. That's not a genuine conversation.

If you're wise, you'll realize that what you know is only a tiny part of all there is to know. You will then remain open to searching for new knowledge through every encounter and every conversation. This is the highest form of wisdom.

During a genuine conversation, you're listening to yourself as carefully as you're listening to the other person. You're responding to each other and reporting back to each other about how your perception is changing, and that leads you both to new questions and new avenues to explore in the conversation. Both participants are shedding their skins, and both come out of it enriched and new. Both parties are pursuing the truth, and both are listening and thinking clearly. Both sense that the conversation is meaningful, interesting, and positive.

You can only have a conversation like that if you assume the person you're listening to knows something that you don't.

*

Rules in Action: Application

"... and I guess that's why I said my husband feels like a stranger to me."

"Does Roger know you feel this way, Sharon?"

"You're the psychologist! You tell me."

"I'm a psychologist, not a psychic." She smiled and paused long enough to allow her patient to add anything else she wanted to say. After a brief silence she continued:

"I hear what you're saying – but don't give up hope. From what I can sense, the two of you still really love each other. You've just forgotten how to have a meaningful conversation – and that can be fixed."

A glimmer of hope showed on Sharon's face for a moment.

"Do you really think so?"

"Yes," replied the psychologist, "But it's going to take some work on your part. You'll have to learn how to be an active listener. I can give you something to read, if you like. But I want to stress the point again: A conversation is a two-way thing. It's not only about how you talk – you also have to listen."

RULE 10:
BE PRECISE IN YOUR SPEECH

Rules in Action: Introduction

In this chapter, Peterson borrows a children's story to illustrate the message behind rule 10. The story is originally by Jack Kent, entitled: *There's No Such Thing as a Dragon*. There's an interesting moral to it, and it goes like this:

Billy Bixbee wakes up one fine morning and discovers there's a friendly, cat-sized dragon on his bed. When he tells his mom and dad about it, they refuse to believe him, of course.

"There's no such thing as a dragon," they insist, even though the evidence starts piling up. The more they deny it, the bigger the dragon grows. Still, they refuse to admit there's a dragon.

Every time the subject comes up, it gets swept under the carpet — and that's not a good place to keep a real, live dragon. There, under the rug, it grows and grows. Soon, it's so big that there's no room left in the house, forcing mom to use the windows to get into each room to vacuum.

Next thing the dragon runs off with the house on its back. When dad gets home from work, there's only an empty space where the house once stood. The mailman tells him where to find the house, and he climbs up and joins his wife and son. But still, nobody admits that the dragon is real.

Billy is at his wit's end at this point in the story. In desperation, he insists on pointing out the facts to his willfully blind parents:

"There really is a dragon!" He keeps saying.

*

Perception is complicated. Through our amazing powers of perception, which science only barely understands, we reduce the unfathomable complexity of the world into a single, meaningful whole – one that makes sense and one that we can believe is real. It's almost like a magic trick.

We assume that when we look out at the world, we see the real things that are in it – but that's not the whole truth. We filter out most of what we see, and **we don't perceive objects without ascribing some kind of meaning to them.** The world is vast, and things are so inter-connected with so many layers of complexity that we need to reduce it all down to: "What does this object mean to me." If it means nothing, it hardly registers in our perception. It's a useful trick of the mind, but it makes us partially blind to a wider truth. We mistakenly think that our perception is complete and sufficient – until the world misbehaves.

When something fundamental goes wrong in our lives, the veneer cracks and we have to face a new and chaotic version of the world. When you drive, for example, your car becomes an extension of you. When it suddenly breaks down, you will find yourself confronting a mystery. You suddenly realize that your car is complicated – it's ability to function smoothly, which you take for granted, depends on even more complexities.

It's even worse when something serious happens – such as illness, betrayal, loss, or the death of a loved one. Then our world falls apart. Ancient biological survival mechanisms kick in, and our body goes into flight or fight mode. The underworld appears with all its monsters and dragons that are hiding under the rug. **What seemed predictable and manageable now seems completely out of control.**

The chaos often collects slowly over time, such as when a family falls apart. Instead of admitting to "the dragon under the rug," all the problems are ignored until they become too big to ignore anymore. That's the lesson we can draw from Billy Bixbee and his dragon.

That's also why it's so important for us to be precise in what we say and how we say it.

If you remain silent, perhaps convincing yourself that you're a good, strong person for doing it, the dragon under the rug grows. If you avoid problems and refuse to investigate or face them, the same thing happens.

By speaking precisely, you can specify what is bothering you. You can bring it out from under the carpet and bring it out into the light. If you fail to define what you want, or what you don't want, success (resolving the problem) becomes vague and impossible.

When you're precise about what's going wrong, it is clearly defined from the millions of things that could have gone wrong but didn't.

Many couples, for example, start out arguing about something specific, only to see the argument evolve into an argument about everything. It's not specific. **You can't solve a universal, unspecified problem.** If you leave things in the murky dark (under the rug), life becomes stagnant and poisonous.

It's better to confront the sea of chaos using precise thought and language. Take aim at the specific monster that appears, and don't sweep it under anything. Be forthright, honest, and clear about who you are and what you want.

*

Rules in Action: Application

As soon as Billy speaks out and makes it crystal clear that the dragon is, in fact, real, it begins to shrink, and soon enough, it's the size of a cat once more.

Mom and Dad are relieved but still as reluctant as ever. While they finally have to admit the truth, Mom is still confused by all of it and asks:

"But why did it have to get quite so big?"

Billy shakes his head in disbelief. He timidly replies: "Maybe it just wanted to be noticed."

RULE 11:
DO NOT BOTHER CHILDREN WHEN THEY ARE SKATEBOARDING

Rules in Action: Introduction

"I can't bear to watch," Vanessa said. Her voice was full of motherly concern. Her 12-year-old son stood perched on a rock high above an icy mountain pool with his little knees knocking together, staring down at where he was intending to jump.

"It will be alright. He can handle it," said Rob, who was shivering slightly from the icy water but smiling and relaxed. "There are no sharp rocks down there; I've checked every inch of the pool. It's safe enough."

"If the fall doesn't kill him, the cold will. I can't bear it. Make him come down from there."

"I'm here if he needs me," said Rob. "But I don't think he needs anyone. He's strong enough — and I think it will be good for him."

"How can you say that? He's only 12! I'm going to tell him to come down right now."

"Leave him be. Don't make him frightened. He needs to know he's not made of glass. Besides, it's not really as high as it looks from up there."

*

There's a latent daredevil inside every kid. We try to make playgrounds safe for children, but if we make them too safe, sooner or later the kids will find a way to make playing riskier and more exciting.

It's the same with adults. Most adults do what they can to provide a safe, secure home, get a steady job, and insulate their families from most of the risks in life. At some point, however, that becomes boring, so **people push the limits a little to keep things exciting and to grow**. There's something inside human beings that makes us want to explore the very edge of chaos – and it's thrilling, even though (or perhaps because) it's dangerous.

Peterson got the title for Rule 11 from watching kids skateboarding outside the university building where he worked. They performed amazing feats of skill and courage on their skateboards, down the steps, on the railings, and onto the cement flower boxes. It was *meant* to be dangerous – and they did it on purpose to become better skaters. But the university administration put up skate-stoppers, making a mess of the building façade and forcing the skaters to move away. There's a subtle lesson in that.

If we try too hard to make life safe and perfect, make everyone equal and agreeable, and eliminate all the natural differences between people, it leads to something even worse. **It robs us of the chance to transcend our limitations and evolve as individuals.**

There's something draconian about people, systems, or ideologies that insist on narrow, rigid codes of behavior using the excuse that it's for our own good. It's not that serious when it pertains to skateboarding, but when it comes to politics and ethics, it gets far more complicated. For example, is it right to insist that boys are forced to be socialized like girls in order to make them more docile?

Peterson calls it "an insidious and profoundly anti-human spirit." People who want to eliminate all conflict and struggle from life are like "self-appointed judges of the human race."

Culture is oppressive by its very nature – it has to be in order to safeguard amidst all the chaos. **It's easy to condemn the mindset of the majority, or label people as patriarchal, oppressive, unfair, or biased.** But that involves forgetting the complexities of the past and the lessons we've learned from them. Even compassion can become a vice. People who avoid conflict and who are full of empathy and compassion often let others walk all over them. Is that wise?

It's our duty to ensure that the wisdom we've inherited from the past is made fit for use in the present. That means leaving room for a little bit of chaos, while walking the fine line between the two extremes.

Despite all our faults, human beings are seriously remarkable creatures. **Give people the benefit of the doubt. Allow them their banter, their competition, and their risk-taking – unless you want a world full of spineless conformists with no imagination.** Not all forms of teasing are malicious. Not all differences between people need to become ammunition for social reform. Don't negate consciousness by interfering with the natural processes that let boys struggle to become men and girls become women.

Leave children alone when they are skateboarding.

*

Rules in Action: Application

"The two of you are going to make me old before my time!" Vanessa said, as she handed a towel to her son. His teeth were chattering, but there was a huge grin on his face.

"Was that worth it? I hope so, because you nearly gave me a heart attack!"

The boy could only nod as he shivered, but it was clear that it had been worth it. Cold as he was, there was a kind of light dancing in his youthful eyes.

Vanessa looked over at Rob, who was also drying himself off. They exchanged a glance that was full of meaning. Rob's smile meant: "I told you so!" and Vanessa's look meant that she admitted she'd been wrong to try to stop the child from jumping – though she would never say it in so many words. Still, she smiled and told her son not to forget his shoes.

It was only much later that day when the two of them were alone and getting ready for bed that she finally said to Rob:

"Thanks for today. I think he's going to handle things at school much better from now on. Perhaps I've been too over-protective of him these past few years."

"Don't worry, love," said Rob. *"That's what I'm here for. He needs both of us."*

RULE 12:
PET A CAT WHEN YOU
ENCOUNTER ONE ON THE STREET

Rules in Action: Introduction

"What's that grin on your face, son? Have you been flirting with the nurses again?"

Joel was sitting in his wheelchair, staring out at the fields beyond the borders of the enclosure. At age 23, he had lost both his legs and nearly died. He should have been miserable, or angry, or both. But he was smiling. His father sat down on the bench not far away. Joel wheeled himself closer so they could talk.

"I haven't seen a nurse in hours," Joel said. "I've been watching the trees dance."

The old man gazed toward a line of trees in the distance. There was a gentle autumn breeze, and the trees swayed this way and that, almost as if they were dancing to some unknown tune. As he watched, he searched his mind for something meaningful to say – but found nothing there, and so they just sat and watched the trees.

*

Although we sometimes find at least a sprinkling of wonder and magic in life, our lives are also inevitably full of **suffering and the limitations of *Being*.** How do we respond to the cold, hard facts of existence?

69

The doctrines of the major religions state it as a given: Humans are fragile, at best, if not hopelessly broken. You will find the same core idea in Buddhism, Christianity, and Judaism – phrased differently, of course. It's hard to disagree, no matter what your beliefs are, and it's reasonable to wonder how on earth we can accept our fragility, let alone be happy about it. **How can we thrive when these are the facts?** Should we even want to continue?

The trials of life can defeat us and make us bitter and angry. But we can learn to transcend them.

In the final chapter, the author shares the heart-wrenching story of his daughter, Mikhaila, and her struggles with severe polyarticular juvenile idiopathic arthritis (JIA). It was one of the hardest things the Peterson family had to deal with. The trouble started when Mikhaila was about six years old. She was taken from one doctor to the next. Finally, a rheumatologist recommended "multiple early joint replacements."

Peterson describes how his daughter **fought bravely to deal with her pain and limitations** over the next two decades. While this was happening, the demands of everyday life did not disappear, so they all had to adjust and learn how to deal with the reality; otherwise, they would have been completely overwhelmed. Peterson's advice:

> *"**Set aside some time to talk and to think about the illness or other crisis and how it should be managed every day. Do not talk or think about it otherwise.** If you do not limit its effect, you will become exhausted, and everything will spiral into the ground. This is not helpful... **the parts of your brain that generate anxiety are more interested in the fact that there is a plan than in the details of the plan.**"*

It's a testament to the human spirit that we can survive pain and loss and come out the other side stronger and wiser. To reach that point, you have to be able to **see the good in *Being*, despite its limitations**. We're not invulnerable superheroes; in fact, there's a deep part of human nature that seems to need limitations.

If you can imagine a being (like God) that is all-powerful, omniscient and omnipresent, what is the one thing such a being is lacking? The answer: Limitations.

The development of the famous comic book hero *Superman* illustrates this well. When the audience first got to know Superman, he was mighty, but he had limitations. Over time, however, as he battled increasingly powerful foes, he became more and more invincible. It was at that point, strangely enough, *Superman* comics became unpopular. **A hero with no challenges is no hero at all**. They had to re-write the story and include kryptonite, giving the superhero a new, all-too-human weakness so that audiences could identify with Superman again.

What it illustrates is that the struggle against our limitations is what ultimately brings meaning to our lives – even though it's painful.

Holding onto the attitude that life sucks, that life is hateful, painful, and meaningless can only make things worse. That pathway leads good people to decisions that willfully inflict pain on others. Such an approach is evil.

How can we manage to say "yes" to life when we feel like saying "no?" When calamity strikes, the mind becomes impotent, and when the worst happens, something deeper than thinking kicks in. How can one outthink a sudden incapacity, a growing incurable disease, or a terminal illness? The only conclusion one yields is that life itself is evil and intolerable. In these instances Peterson advises **not to *think* but to *notice* instead. Instead of trying to make sense of the intolerable pain and suffering, deal with it courageously, every single day and try to notice and see the good around you.**

For this very reason, the author makes a point of petting cats (dogs too) when meeting them in the street. The real question is: What can you do to bring a little more light, a little more acceptance, and a little more wonder into your life? It doesn't need to be a huge thing — petting a cat is a good start.

If you're out on a walk to clear your head and a cat decides that you're worthy enough to rub up against your leg, it's a mini-reminder that life contains a bit of wonder too. **It makes the suffering just a bit more bearable.**

*

Rules in Action: Application

"I'm proud of you, Joel, my son." The old man wiped his eyes and looked away into the distance once more.

Joel said nothing, but felt his father's hand reach for his own and squeeze hard. That was as far as his father would go – he was never the most demonstrative man. But Joel knew that it was real, and that was enough.

"In a way, losing my legs has been a blessing," Joel finally said. "I can't remember the last time I've had the chance to just sit and look at how miraculous everything is."

His father, still silent, nodded in agreement.

CONCLUSION

Chaos, on the one hand, and order on the other. These two opposing principles are constants in our lives, and each of us has to figure out, on our own, how to best navigate the path between them.

It's never easy, and sometimes it's downright torturous, especially if you refuse to look away from the truth and remain brave and authentic enough to listen to your conscience speaking from the murky depths of the soul. We all have to learn about our own faults. It is only when we can do this with courage and honesty that the truth is revealed and the way forward becomes clear. If we don't, we get stuck repeating the same painful mistakes.

Is it possible to turn yourself into someone you admire? Can you rely on yourself? Will you choose to go against the stream, putting aside all laziness and lack of honor and struggle to become the kind of person who makes life a little more like Heaven and a little less like Hell?

That's the goal that underpins the 12 Rules for Life.

It's always tempting to give in to chaos. It's tempting to just give up. But experience teaches us that it's not better.

Stand up straight and face life as if you mean it. That's a better alternative. Treat yourself as if you deserve your best efforts. Tell the truth, especially to yourself, and set your own house in order.

When you approach life in this way, doors of opportunity will open. You will be less of a burden to yourself and to those who love and care for you. Choose your own set of rules and stick to them until you find ones that make more sense – but don't let it go.

This is the only true antidote for chaos.

***

If you would like to listen to this summary, you can follow the link below to join Audible.com and get the audiobook for free.

Follow the steps below to instantly access your free summary audiobook:

1) **Open** your smart phone's camera application
2) **Aim** your phone's camera **and focus on** the QR Code below

3) **Click** the link that pops up on the top side of your screen

You can also follow this link: **http://bit.ly/adb-12rules**

Gift: Guided Challenge

"What is your friend: the things you know, or the things you don't know. First of all, there's a lot more things you don't know. And second, the things you don't know is the birthplace of all your new knowledge! So if you make the things you don't know your friend, rather than the things you know, well then you're always on a quest in a sense. You're always looking for new information in the off chance that somebody who doesn't agree with you will tell you something you couldn't have figured out on your own! It's a completely different way of looking at the world. It's the antithesis of opinionated."

– Jordan B. Peterson

Now is the time to implement all that you have learned in this summary towards your life and professional goals! We know the overwhelming feeling of grappling with the wealth of information you now carry... analyzing it, compartmentalizing it, and then applying it. To kill that tiny but overwhelming monster while it's small, we went ahead and formulated a **30-Day Guided Challenge to gradually ease you into massive action**. In the Guided Challenge, you will:

- Implement simple principles that instantly increase your confidence and effectiveness in any social interaction

- Uncover your deepest values and become more self-aware

- Initiate a personalized process to add more purpose and meaning to your life

- Understand how to bring more clarity to your close relationships and attract quality people to your inner circle

Think of the Guided Challenge as the last excuse on your shelf. After reading the guide you simply have no excuses holding you back from implementing the insights of this book to your life.

Follow the steps below to instantly access your exclusive 30-Day Guided Challenge:

1) **Open** your smart phone's camera application

2) **Aim** your phone's camera **and focus on** the QR Code below

3) **Click** the link that pops up on the top side of your screen

You can also download the Guided Challenge by visiting the following link: **https://exegrowth.com/pdfguide-12rfl-04**

If you downloaded **Power Insights** at the start of the summary check your inbox, the **Guided Challenge** awaits you.

Our team at Executive**Growth** cannot thank you enough for believing in our work and trusting us to deliver the wisdom within *12 Rules for Life* directly to you.

> *The mission of our team is to increase the productivity and widen the perspective of our readers' lives by providing the most comprehensive, entertaining, and actionable summaries of powerful works.*

If you feel that we have done right by our mission, please leave a review on Amazon by visiting the following link **<http://bit.ly/egreview>**.

It takes <u>less than one minute</u> to leave a <u>one-sentence</u> review, which will make a material impact on our ability to write <u>more summaries for you, your friends and family</u>. Don't you think you and your friends and family deserve great summary books? Do it for you. Do it for them... and do it for our struggling writer & founder, Carlos. ☺

You can also scan the QR code below to leave a review (follow the same steps as the previous QR code):

If you do not feel we met our mission or can improve we would love to hear from you too! We are always trying to make your experience better and your feedback is pivotal in the process – don't hold back any punches; we're pretty tough. Please leave your feedback by visiting the following link **<http://exegrowth.com/feedback>**.

We hold you in the highest regard for investing in yourself. We are committed to staying your companions in this exciting yet challenging journey of personal growth. **Let's go and let's grow!**

Links

Audiobook Summary: http://bit.ly/adb-12rules

12 Rules for Life **Full Book:** https://amzn.to/2KDSzK3

Power Insights & Guided Challenge:
https://www.exegrowth.com/pdfguide-12rfl-04

Amazon Review: http://bit.ly/egreview

ExecutiveGrowth Feedback: http://exegrowth.com/feedback

Notes: Capture Your Thoughts

_____
_____
_____
_____
_____
_____
_____
_____
_____
_____
_____
_____
_____
_____
_____
_____
_____
_____
_____
_____
_____
_____

Made in the USA
Monee, IL
14 March 2020